Name: ______________________________

Class: ______________________________

Teacher: ______________________________

Islamic Studies Workbook Level 2

Minhaj-ul-Quran International

Published by
Minhaj-ul-Quran Publications
30 Brindley Road
Manchester
M16 9HQ (UK)

Compiled by
Kirren Ahmed Amin and Safina Nazir

Edited by
Waqas Amin

Design and Typeset
Waqas Amin

ISBN: 978-1-913553-01-2

www.minhajpublications.com

www.islamforkids.org.uk

First published January 2020

Printed in the UK

Islamic Studies Workbook Level 2

Workbook Compilers

Kirren Ahmed Amin

Safina Nazir

Workbook Editor

Waqas Amin

Minhaj-ul-Quran International

Preface

In the name of Allah, the Most Merciful, the Most Kind.

WE PRAISE ALLAH ﷻ that the Muslim community has come a long way since the days when the first immigrants settled in Britain. From that time till today, there have been significant developments in the quality of educational material being produced by British Muslims. Many advancements have been made in this regard such that English is fast becoming one of the academic languages of Islam, alongside Arabic, Persian, Urdu and Turkish.

The importance of education cannot be overstated. The British Muslim community has put great effort into imparting Islamic knowledge to their children. Islamic classes and religious seminaries have been established up and down the country for the single goal of teaching the coming generations the fundamentals of their religion. Among those that have been at the forefront in this regard is Minhaj-ul-Quran International, a global organisation with branches in over 90 countries.

As an organisation, Minhaj-ul-Quran International seeks to uplift Muslims worldwide through the revival of education and spirituality. It established its first branch in the United Kingdom in the late 1980s and founded its first centre in the 1990s. For more than two decades it has endeavoured to provide for the educational and spiritual needs of the Muslim diaspora of Great Britain.

The 'Islam for Kids' initiative is part of the longstanding services of Minhaj-ul-Quran International. This Islamic Studies series was produced and developed by second and third generation British scholars, who are trained classically in the traditional Islamic sciences, alongside QTS (Qualified Teaching Status) accredited teachers. It is an indigenous and local endeavour by the UK branch of Minhaj-ul-Quran International to fulfil the educational needs of native English-speaking students.

The Syllabus

The 'Islam for Kids' Islamic Studies series has been split into six levels with each level corresponding to the years of the state-funded education system in the UK. It is recommended to start level one at the age of 5 when the child starts year one at primary school and to complete level 6 by the age of 11 when the child completes his or her primary school education. However, the series can be started earlier at an earlier age or later depending on the ability of the student.

The six levels have been grouped into three stages, with each stage consisting of two levels. In the first stage, which consists of levels one and two, the aim is to ease the child into understanding Islamic concepts and terminology. The purpose of this stage is not to burden the child with technical knowledge about Islam, but rather to simply instil in them a sense of Muslim identity and to explore key Islamic concepts.

Traditionally, Muslim parents have been advised to have a play-based approach with their children's learning for the first seven years and then to formally teach them for the next seven years. Following this advice, in the first two years of the syllabus, a more visual approach has been adopted with the text being kept at a minimum. This enables the content to be taught in a child-friendly manner and allows teachers and parents to make the lessons more interactive and engaging for the child.

The second stage of the syllabus begins at level three when the child reaches seven years of age. From this level onwards, a more formal approach to learning is adopted. Many of the concepts in the first stage are revisited, but instead of being largely pictorial, they are more text-based so that the key concepts can be conveyed in detail to the child and to encourage the child to start thinking about the content in more depth.

In the third stage of the syllabus, which consists of levels five and six, the series shifts to a more text-heavy approach. This is to encourage the child to learn independently and practice their key reading and comprehension skills. The content at this level increases in difficulty to engage students academically and to raise the standard of literacy and understanding of Islamic concepts.

The concepts from the previous two stages are revisited in this third stage but in much more detail. Parents and teachers alike will find this stage beneficial as reading material to help prepare in terms of subject knowledge for teaching the lessons in the earlier two stages. In this way, the three stages work together to ease the child into becoming well acquainted with Islamic terminology, concepts and values.

By the end of this syllabus, the child will have acquired the essential Islamic knowledge (*Fard `Ayn*) for them to be able to live their life as a practising Muslim. This Islamic Studies series is an excellent resource for parents to lay the foundation for their child's learning. If Allah ﷻ wills, further levels will be added to this syllabus, thus enhancing the child's understanding of Islam and enabling them to become lifelong learners of the Islamic tradition.

The Workbooks

The workbooks were developed to support the delivery of the textbooks. It is an invaluable resource for teachers. The purpose of the workbooks is not to test the content of the textbooks, but to reinforce terminology and concepts through active learning. The workbooks follow the same pattern as the textbooks and thus can be used alongside them to engage the content in a manner that is appealing to children.

Teachers are advised to go through the content of the lesson first by reading through the textbook and explaining the terminology and concepts to the learner. The teacher should have a dialogue with the learner and through simple yes and no questions ensure that the content of the lesson is properly understood. Once the teacher is confident that the learner understands the content properly, he or she should then engage the workbooks.

Each lesson can be broken down according to the activities. Before the learner starts the activity, the teacher should review it first and explain it to the learner verbally. Instructions have been provided to assist in this regard. It is advised for the teacher to reinforce the terminology and concepts before the learner undertakes the activity. Doing this will ensure that the learner can undertake the activity independently and the activity is not done in vain.

After completing the activity, some time should be given to the learner to reflect over their work by discussing their answers with a partner. Whether as an individual or as a class, there must be feedback to ensure that the learner has understood the lesson. The purpose of the activity is not to test the learner's knowledge, but to reinforce the content he or she has learnt. It is a teaching tool to help teachers recognise where a learner needs further assistance. It is essential, through the process of feedback, that the teacher provides the learner with the extra guidance needed to understand the content adequately. Learning objectives have been provided at the beginning of each lesson for this end.

After completing the activities, several key words have been provided for each lesson. These key words are important vocabulary, which the learner should learn and memorise. It aims to support the learner's literacy and develop their vocabulary. For high ability learners, they can write sentences for each word or write a short passage containing all the words. Doing so will help solidify the lesson in their minds.

At the end of each lesson, a lesson summary has been provided. The purpose of the lesson summary is to help bring the lesson to a close by reviewing the key concepts. Doing this will help reinforce the lesson. Teachers must not just aimlessly go through the activities one by one, but instead, give some thought and deliberation to each of them. The teacher must engage the student through discussions; the mechanism of feedback is an important tool for achieving this. It is the teacher's responsibility to ensure that the learners have achieved the learning objective.

Teachers must plan and familiarise themselves with the textbooks and activities. It is important to engage the learners constantly. Engaging the learner and being concerned for them is the secret to becoming a successful teacher. These children are a sacred trust from Allah ﷾, and it is our duty collectively as teachers and parents to dispense with this trust in the best manner possible. The future of our *Ummah* depends on the calibre of children we raise today. May Allah ﷾ give us the divine enablement (*tawfiq*) to dispense with this trust as it duly deserves.

Final Words

We are eager to hear from the wider community and to gain feedback regarding the series. For this purpose, we have set up an email address for you to send us your feedback. You can contact us at the following address: **feedback@fmriuk.org**.

Finally, I would like to thank Kirren Ahmed Amin and Safina Nazir for compiling the workbooks, and Ajmal Khan and Rayhan Khan for their assistance in design. I pray to Allah ﷾ that He accepts our efforts and makes it a means of salvation for us in this life and the next, and we pray that this series becomes a means of uplifting the *Ummah* for generations to come.

Amin bi-jahi Sayyid al-Mursalin ﷺ.

Waqas Amin
Deputy Director
Farid-e-Millat Research Institute (FMRI-UK)
19th Rabi` ath-Thani 1441 AH/16th December 2019 CE

Contents

Islamic Studies
Level 2

1. MY DIN (WAY OF LIFE)

Lesson Objective: To Understand Islam, Iman and Ihsan.

ISLAM

INSTRUCTIONS: Label each pillar, draw a picture and write a short description for each.

There are five pillars of Islam, which are important for every Muslim to perform. They are:

1. ______________________

____
____
____
____
____
____

2. ______________________

____
____
____
____
____
____

3. ______________________________

4. ______________________________

5. ______________________________

IMAN

INSTRUCTIONS: For each pillar, fill in the gap and colour in the picture.

1. We believe in

____

2. We believe in the

____

3. We believe in the

____

4. We believe in the

____

5. We believe in

____

6. We believe in

____

7. We believe in the

____

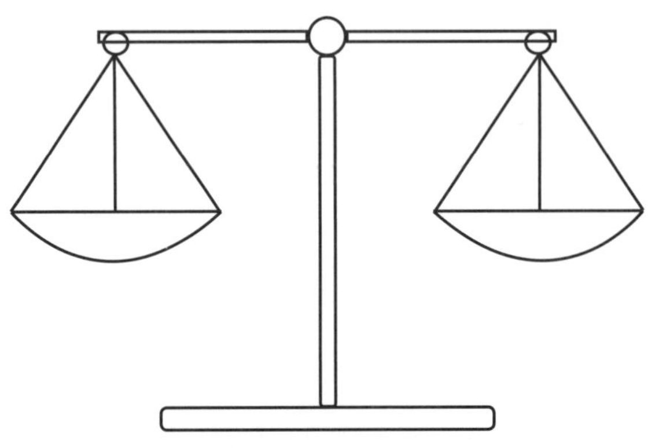

IHSAN

INSTRUCTIONS: Colour in the picture and write a short description about Ihsan.

Ihsan is...

____

____

KEY WORDS

Din	Islam	Iman	Ihsan
Shahadah	Salah	Sawm	Zakah
Hajj	Allah	Prophets	Day of Judgement

LESSON SUMMARY

- There are five pillars of Islam which are important for every Muslim to perform; they are: Shahadah, Salah, Sawm, Zakah and Hajj.
- As Muslims, we believe in seven important things. We believe in Allah, the Angels, the Holy books, Prophets, Life After Death, all good and bad comes from Allah and the Day of Judgement.
- Ihsan is our relationship with Allah. It means we remember Allah every day and knows that He sees what we do all the time.

2. CLEANLINESS

Lesson Objective: To Understand the Importance of Keeping Clean.

INSTRUCTIONS: Draw three pictures under each heading to show how to keep clean. Write a short description for each.

Cleanliness is very important for Muslims. We should try to keep ourselves and everything around us clean. We can do this by....

1. KEEPING MYSELF CLEAN

2. KEEPING MY HOUSE CLEAN

3. KEEPING MY SCHOOL CLEAN

ACTIVITY

INSTRUCTIONS: Sit with a partner; each one names a different way to keep themselves and the things around them clean. When one person can't think of something, the other wins!

KEY WORDS

Clean	Wash	Soap	Flush
Shower	Wipe	Comb	Tidy

LESSON SUMMARY

- Keeping ourselves clean is very important.
- We should keep ourselves clean all the time.
- We should keep everything around us clean, especially when we are at home or school.
- Some ways we can keep clean is by flushing the toilet, cleaning the toilet after use and washing our hands with soap.
- We should have a bath or shower regularly, comb our hair and keep tidy.
- We should brush our teeth twice a day, wash our hands before and after eating, and wash our hands after touching anything dirty.

3. KEEPING SAFE

Lesson Objective: To Understand How to Keep Ourselves Safe.

INSTRUCTIONS: Sort out the pictures from the cut-out section and put them in the right columns. Write a small sentence for each picture. Then discuss in pairs how these things either keep us safe or not safe.

KEEPING SAFE

NOT KEEPING SAFE

INSTRUCTIONS: Colour in the signs for crossing the road. Then discuss with your teacher the safe way to cross the road.

KEY WORDS

Safe	Unsafe	Wait	Traffic lights
Sharp	Hot	Crossing	Car

LESSON SUMMARY

- We should not hurt ourselves and other people.
- We should look after ourselves and be careful.
- We should listen to our teachers and parents and do what they tell us.
- We should not hide anything from them, especially if it is bad.
- The road is dangerous. We need to be careful when we are crossing the road and look both ways when we are crossing the road.
- We should be careful with hot things and things that use electricity.

4. THE MIRACLE OF COMMANDING THE RAIN

Lesson Objective: To Understand the Miracle of Commanding the Rain.

INSTRUCTIONS: Match the two parts of the sentences together from each column.

1. Life was hard in Madinah because...	... to pray for rain.
2. A man stood up and asked the Prophet ﷺ ...	... there was a lot of rain.
3. The Prophet ﷺ prayed to Allah سبحانه وتعالى to send rain...	... it did not rain.
4. The homes were getting damaged because...	... to send the rain around them and not on them.
5. So the Prophet ﷺ asked Allah سبحانه وتعالى ...	... and it started to rain a lot.

INSTRUCTIONS: Colour in the picture and draw rain clouds to show the rain around Madinah.

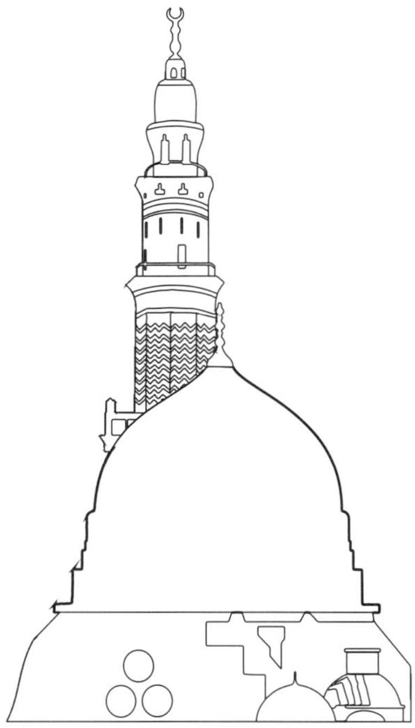

KEY WORDS

Miracle	Rain	Madinah	Water
Prayed	Mosque	Sky	Cloud

LESSON SUMMARY

- A miracle is a special sign that Allah ﷻ gives to Prophets to show they are speaking the truth.
- Life was hard in Madinah because there was no water to drink.
- A man asked the Prophet Muhammad ﷺ to pray for rain.
- The Prophet ﷺ raised his hands to pray and it rained for a whole week.
- The following week the same man asked the Prophet ﷺ to pray the rain stops as their homes were getting damaged.
- The Prophet ﷺ prayed for the rain to be sent around them and not on them.
- As soon as the Prophet ﷺ prayed, the rain moved away from the city.
- It was still raining around the city and the people were happy with the well needed rain.

5. KALIMAH TAYYIBAH

Lesson Objective: To Understand the Kalimah Tayyibah.

INSTRUCTIONS: Colour the boxes that describe Allah ﷻ correctly in green and the boxes that do not in red.

Allah is the one true God.	Allah has a wife.
Allah has children.	Allah made everything.
Allah is not a boy or a girl.	Allah needs us.
Allah is an idol.	Allah was not born.
Allah is like us.	Allah sees and hears everything.

INSTRUCTIONS: Colour in the Arabic text and write down the English translation.

Kalimah Tayyibah (The Pure Word)

لَآ إِلٰهَ إِلَّا اللّٰهُ

مُحَمَّدٌ رَّسُولُ اللّٰهِ

EXTENSION: Memorise the Arabic text and the English translation.

INSTRUCTIONS: Write four things about Prophet Muhammad ﷺ.

He is ______________________________

____

____

He is ______________________________

____

____

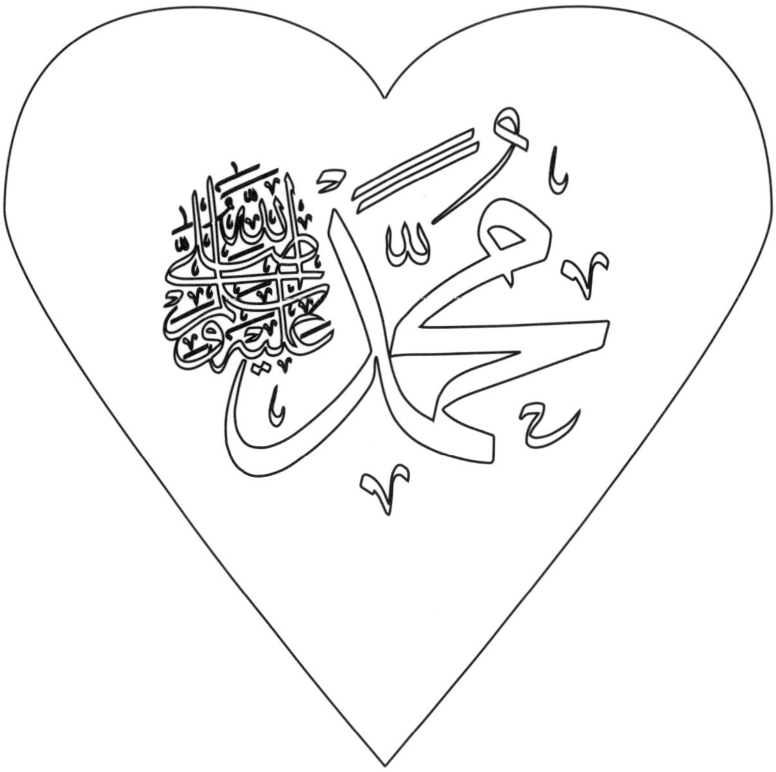

Prophet Muhammad ﷺ

He is ______________________________

____

____

He is ______________________________

____

____

KEY WORDS

Believe	God	Messenger	Prophet
Partner	Beloved	Final	Example

LESSON SUMMARY

- The Kalimah Tayyibah tells us what we believe about Allah ﷻ and Prophet Muhammad ﷺ.
- The Kalimah Tayyibah means: There is no God but Allah and Muhammad is the Messenger of Allah.
- We believe in Allah ﷻ. Allah ﷻ is the name of the one true God.
- Allah ﷻ made everything and Allah ﷻ does not have any family.
- Allah ﷻ is the greatest and the most powerful.
- We believe in the Prophet Muhammad ﷺ. He is Allah's final Prophet and Messenger. He is the leader of all the Prophets and is the best human.
- Prophet Muhammad ﷺ is Allah's best creation and is an example and guide for all people.

6. WUDU'

Lesson Objective: To Know the Actions of Wudu' in the Correct Order.

INSTRUCTIONS: Fill in the gaps and number the pictures in the right order.

Wudu' is an important way to keep ____________.

We need to do wudu' to __________ and to touch the ___________.

Qur'an	Pray	Clean

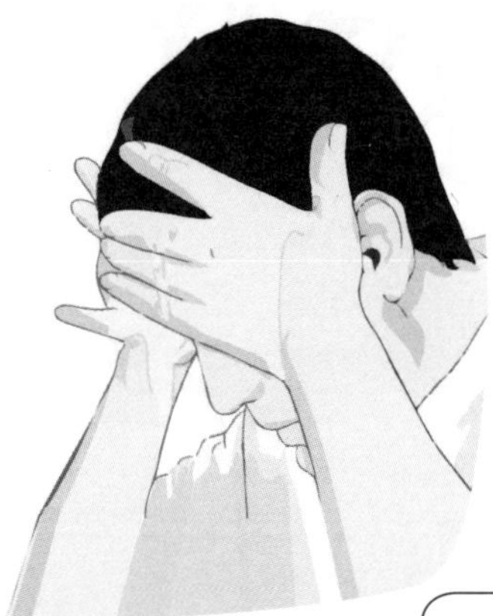

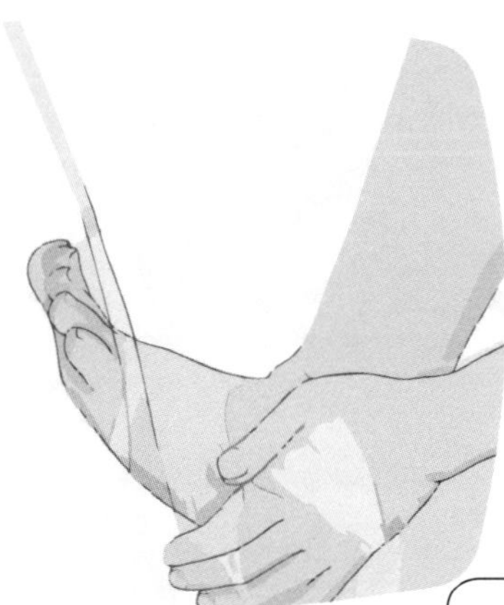

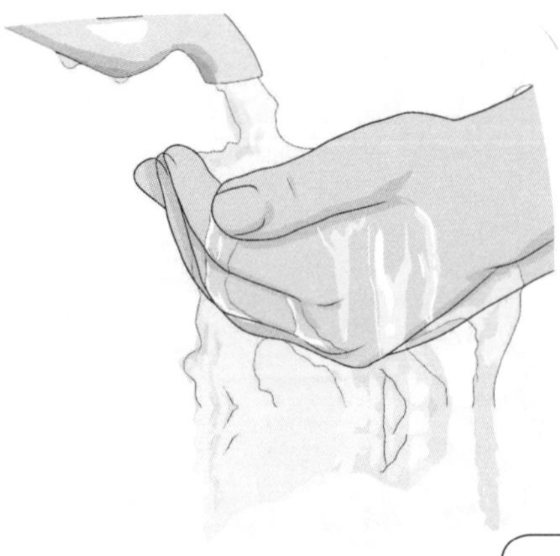

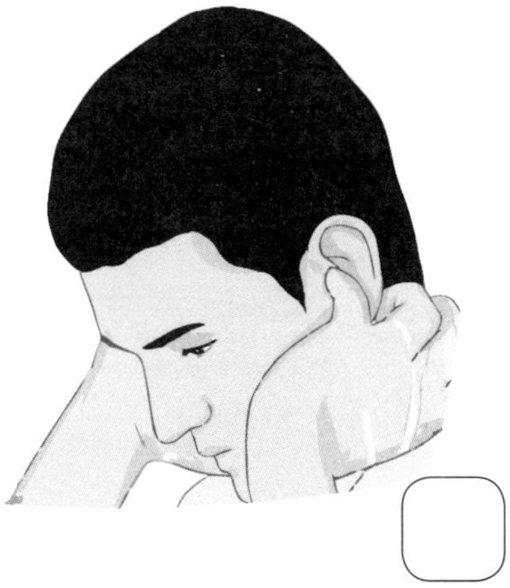

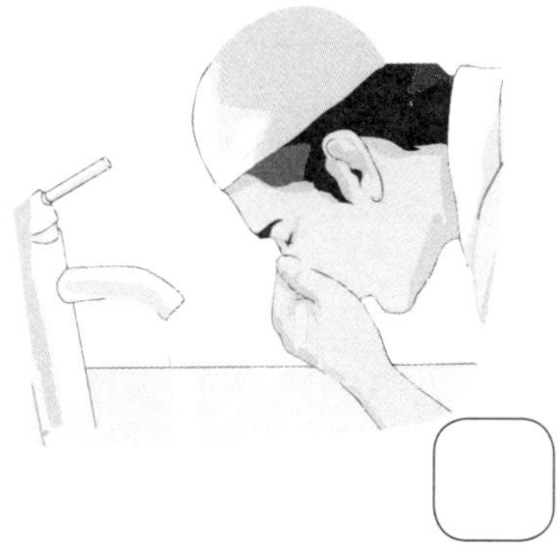

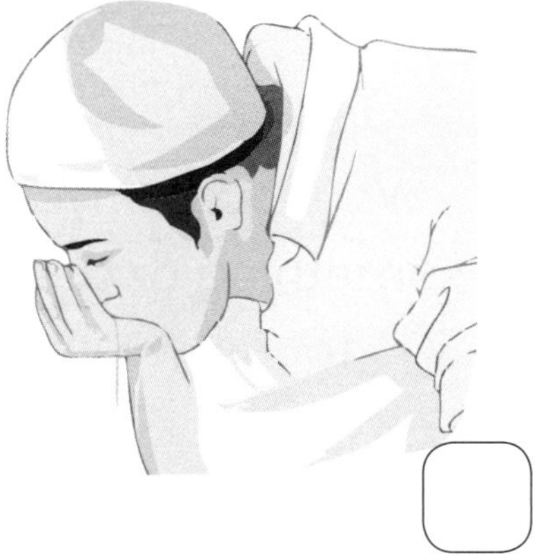

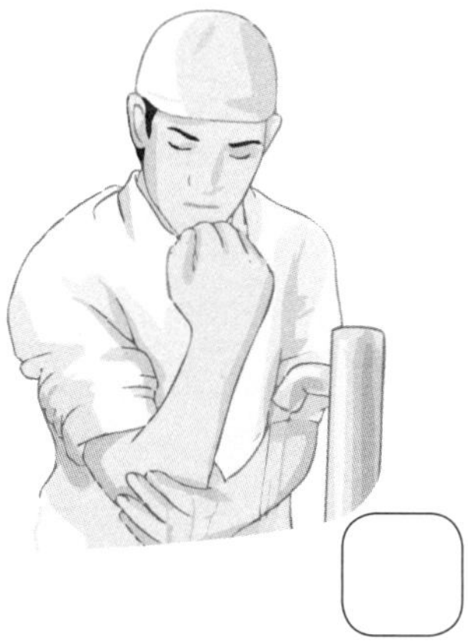

EXTENSION: For each of the pictures write a short description.

KEY WORDS

Wash	Wipe	Face	Arms
Head	Feet	Ears	Nose

LESSON SUMMARY

- Wudu' is an important way to keep clean.
- We need to do wudu' to pray and to touch the Qur'an.
- We perform wudu' in the correct order.

7. GOOD MANNERS

Lesson Objective: To Understand the Importance of Good Manners for a Muslim.

INSTRUCTIONS: Fill in the speech bubble with the right phrase.

Whenever we ask for something we should say:

Whenever anyone gives us something or does something for us, we should say:

Whenever we want to ask something from somebody, we should say:

If we accidently do something wrong to somebody, we should say:

INSTRUCTIONS: Design a poster on good manners. You can include do's and don'ts for a Muslim.

KEY WORDS

Please	Thank-you	Sorry	Excuse Me
Good Manners	Smile	Kind	Helpful

LESSON SUMMARY

- It is important for Muslims to have good manners.
- A Muslim who has bad manners is not a good person.
- Prophet Muhammed ﷺ had the best manners. He was sent by Allah ﷻ to teach everyone good manners.
- Having good manners means being good to everybody.
- Allah ﷻ does not like people who are rude and behave badly.

8. PROPHET YUNUS عليه السلام

Lesson Objective: To Understand that Prophet Yunus عليه السلام was a Prophet of Allah سبحانه وتعالى.

INSTRUCTIONS: Read the sentences and number them in the correct order. The first and last have been done for you.

Allah سبحانه وتعالى sent Prophet Yunus عليه السلام to Ninevah because they worshipped idols.	1
During the storm, to stop the ship sinking, they had to throw one person in the sea.	
After Prophet Yunus عليه السلام left, his people asked Allah سبحانه وتعالى for forgiveness.	
He tried to make the people believe, but they did not listen.	
Prophet Yunus عليه السلام saw this as a sign and jumped off; a whale swallowed him.	
When Prophet Yunus عليه السلام went on a ship, there was a huge storm.	
Prophet Yunus عليه السلام was chosen as the one to be thrown off the ship.	
After forty days, the whale dropped off Prophet Yunus عليه السلام near the land.	8

INSTRUCTIONS: Draw a picture of a whale in the sea and write something important that you have learnt from the story of Prophet Yunus عليه السلام.

KEY WORDS

Whale	Ship	Storm	Forgiveness

LESSON SUMMARY

- Allah ﷻ sent Prophet Yunus عليه السلام to Ninevah because they worshipped idols. He tried to make the people believe, but they did not listen.
- Prophet Yunus عليه السلام left and the people asked Allah ﷻ for forgiveness.
- Prophet Yunus عليه السلام went on a ship. There was a huge storm. They had to throw one person in the sea to stop the ship sinking. Prophet Yunus عليه السلام was chosen.
- Prophet Yunus عليه السلام saw this as a sign and jumped off. A whale swallowed him. After forty days, the whale dropped off Prophet Yunus عليه السلام near the land.

9. THE MIRACLE OF CREATING WATER

Lesson Objective: To Understand the Miracle of Creating Water by Prophet Muhammad ﷺ.

INSTRUCTIONS: Fill in the gaps using the wordbank at the bottom of the page.

A miracle is a special sign that Allah ﷻ gives to Prophets to show that they are speaking the truth.

The Prophet ______________ ﷺ is a special prophet. One day there was no _____________ left to drink. There was one small pot with a little bit of water.

Prophet Muhammad ﷺ put his ______________ inside the pot. The water started _____________ and bubbling inside the pot. It started flowing out from the sides of the pot.

The ________________ saw this miracle. "Look! The water is ______________ between the Prophet's fingers like ______________!" they cried.

Fountains	Hand	Muhammad
Companions	Water	Flowing
	Moving	

INSTRUCTIONS: Colour in the picture below. Then write a sentence about something you have learnt from this lesson.

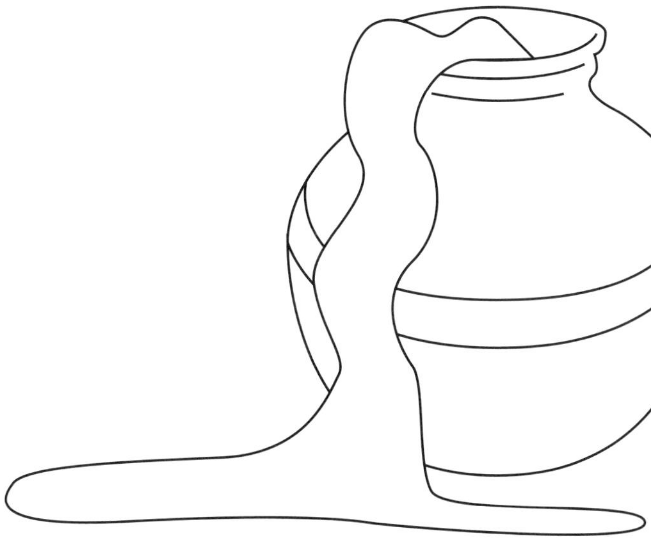

____

____

____

KEY WORDS

Miracle	Water	Companions	Create

LESSON SUMMARY

- A miracle is a special sign that Allah ﷻ gives to Prophets to show they are speaking the truth.
- The miracle of creating water was given to Prophet Muhammad ﷺ from Allah ﷻ.
- When Prophet Muhammad ﷺ put his hand in the pot, the water started moving and bubbling inside the pot. It then came up slowly and started flowing out from the sides of the pot like a running stream.
- The Companions saw this amazing miracle.

10. PROPHETS

Lesson Objective: To Understand Why Prophets are Important in Islam.

INSTRUCTIONS: Colour the boxes that are correct in green and the boxes that are wrong in red.

Prophets are sent by Allah to guide people.	Prophets have no knowledge.
Prophets do not listen to Allah.	Prophets are the best humans.
Prophets lead people to the Hellfire	Muslims believe in the Prophets.
Prophets show people the right way.	Prophets do not believe in Allah
Prophets can do miracles.	Prophets are not special people.

INSTRUCTIONS: Fill in the crossword.

1 down The Prophet who built the Ka`bah.

2 down The Prophet who built the Ark.

3 down The Prophet who was sent to fight against Pharaoh.

3 across The last and final Prophet of Allah سبحانه وتعالى.

4 down He was the first Prophet and the first man.

5 across The Prophet who was raised up to Paradise and was saved by Allah سبحانه وتعالى.

INSTRUCTIONS: Fill in the blanks.

As Muslims, we must:

B_______________ in all the Prophets.

L____________ all the Prophets.

R_______________ the Prophets.

I love the Prophets because:

____

KEY WORDS

Miracles	Knowledge	Respect	Believe
Love	Guide	Special	Right Way

LESSON SUMMARY

- Prophets were sent to guide people.
- As Muslims, we believe, love and respect the Prophets.
- Prophets do not disobey Allah سبحانه وتعالى they are special people.
- Prophets can do miracles and Allah سبحانه وتعالى gave them special knowledge.
- Prophets were sent to different parts of the world.
- Prophets tell people to worship Allah سبحانه وتعالى. They show people the right way.

11. THE SALAH (PRAYER)

Lesson Objective: To Know the Timings of the Five Daily Prayers and the Positions of the Prayer.

INSTRUCTIONS: Match the Arabic terms for the five daily prayers to their English translation. You can colour the boxes with matching colours.

Fajr (فجر)	The Afternoon Prayer
Zuhr (ظهر)	The Late Afternoon Prayer
\`Asr (عصر)	The Dawn Prayer
Maghrib (مغرب)	The Night Prayer
\`Isha’ (عشاء)	The Evening Prayer

INSTRUCTIONS: Label the five daily prayers in the right order.

1.______________________________

The ________________________ Prayer

2.______________________________

The ________________________ Prayer

3.______________________________

The ________________________ Prayer

4.______________________________

The ________________________ Prayer

5.______________________________

The ________________________ Prayer

INSTRUCTIONS: Design your own prayer mat.

INSTRUCTIONS: Put the positions of the prayer in the right order and label them correctly. The pictures are available in the cut-out section.

1.______________________________

2.______________________________

3.______________________________

4.______________________________

5.________________________________

6.________________________________

7.________________________________

8.________________________________

9.______________________________

KEY WORDS

Salah	Fajr	Zuhr	\`Asr
Maghrib	\`Isha'	Takbir at-Tahrimah	Qiyam
Ruku\`	Qawmah	Sajdah	Jalsah
Qa'dah	Salam		

LESSON SUMMARY

- We pray to Allah ﷻ. The Arabic word for prayer is 'Salah' and it is one of the five pillars of Islam.
- We pray five times a day. The Salah names are Fajr, Zuhr, \`Asr, Maghrib and \`Isha'. They are prayed at different times of the day.
- The Prophet Muhammad ﷺ taught us to pray in a certain way and there are different positions we need to follow in the Salah.
- Fajr is the dawn prayer. Zuhr is the afternoon prayer. \`Asr is the late afternoon prayer. Maghrib is the evening prayer and \`Isha' is the night prayer.

12. BEING POLITE

Lesson Objective: To Understand What Being Polite Means as a Muslim.

INSTRUCTIONS: Circle the pictures where the child is being polite.

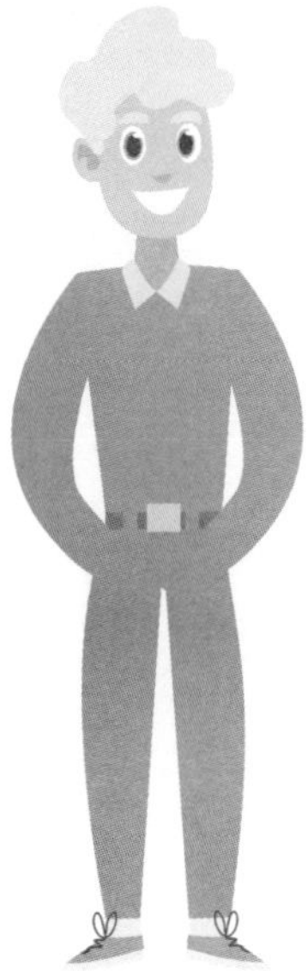

Smiling

Not Smiling

Spitting Out Food

Eating Calmly

Snatching Something and Taking Without Permission

Waiting Patiently

On Time for School

Late to School

INSTRUCTIONS: Give two examples of how to be polite. Write a sentence for each and draw a picture.

Being polite means...

1.________________________________

____

____

____

2.________________________________

____

____

____

Allah ﷻ loves those who are ____________________.

KEY WORDS

Polite	Nice	Kind	Smile
Listen	Respectful	Behave	Patient

LESSON SUMMARY

- Allah ﷻ loves people who are polite.
- We can do lots of things to be polite.
- Being polite means that you are nice to each other and that you do things in the right way.
- A Muslim should always be polite.

13. THE STORY OF `UZAYR عليه السلام

Lesson Objective: To Understand the Story of `Uzayr and Allah's Power.

INSTRUCTIONS: Put the story of `Uzayr عليه السلام in the correct order and draw a picture for each part of the story. The storyboard can be found in the cut-out section.

1

2

3

4	
5	
6	

INSTRUCTIONS: Colour in the text below and draw some pictures in the empty boxes to show that Allah سبحانه وتعالى has power over everything.

KEY WORDS

Life	Angel of Death	Power	Sleep
Food	Donkey	Changed	Back to Life

LESSON SUMMARY

- `Uzayr sat under the tree and wondered what happened to this place. "This place is so empty and broken. How will Allah make this busy and full of life again?" he asked.
- As soon as `Uzayr said these words, Allah sent the Angel of Death to take his life.
- After 100 years the same place was busy and lots of people lived there.
- Allah sent another angel to bring him back to life. The angel told `Uzayr he was asleep for 100 years. He was shocked. His food was still fresh. He was amazed at the power of Allah.
- Allah bought `Uzayr's donkey back to life too. `Uzayr said, "Allah has power over everything".

14. THE MIRACLE OF THE CRYING TREE TRUNK

Lesson Objective: To Understand the Miracle of the Crying Tree Trunk.

READING COMPREHENSION

When Prophet Muhammad ﷺ moved to Madinah, the Prophet's mosque was built. It was a very simple mosque made of mud and bricks. There were no windows or doors.

1. **What was the mosque made from?**

   Wood ☐
   Mud and bricks ☐
   Straw ☐

Tree trunks from date palm trees were used as pillars to hold the building up and the branches of the trees were used as a roof.

In this mosque, Prophet Muhammad ﷺ used to give talks to the people and while he did this, he would lean on the trunk of one of the date palm trees.

2. **What would Prophet Muhammed ﷺ lean on?**

   House ☐
   Person ☐
   Trunk of a palm tree ☐

After a while, a pulpit was made by the Companions so that the Prophet ﷺ could sit down and give his talk. A pulpit is a special chair for the person who is giving a talk to the people.

3. **What is the special chair called?**

   ____

When the Prophet ﷺ started to use the new pulpit, everyone heard the sound of crying. They were surprised and looked around to see where it was coming from. The sound was coming from the trunk of the date palm tree that the Prophet ﷺ used to lean on. The tree trunk was crying!

4. **How do you think the tree trunk felt?**

____

5. **Copy a sentence that makes you think that.**

____

6. **Fill in the blanks using the wordbank below to finish the story.**

Prophet Muhammad ﷺ felt ____________ for the tree trunk. He got off the pulpit and went to the tree trunk. He patted the tree trunk and put his ___________ around it.

The tree trunk stopped ____________ in the same way that a baby stops crying when its mother picks it up.

If the Prophet ﷺ did not make the crying tree trunk feel ____________, it would not have stopped crying, and it would have still been crying ____________.

Prophet Muhammad ﷺ spoke to the tree and said, "I give you a ____________ of either becoming a ____________ tree again or becoming a tree in ____________." The tree trunk chose to be a tree in Paradise, so it was buried by the Companions in the mosque.

Choice	Sorry	Young	Arms
Paradise	Crying	Better	Today

7. **What did you learn from this story about loving Prophet Muhammad ﷺ?**

____

____

INSTRUCTIONS: Draw a picture of the date palm tree in Paradise (Jannah).

KEY WORDS

Miracle	Crying	Palm Tree	Trunk
Pulpit	Paradise	Mosque	Buried

LESSON SUMMARY

- Prophet Muhammad ﷺ used to give talks to the people and while he did this, he would lean on the trunk of one of the date palm trees.
- After a while, a pulpit was made by the Companions so that the Prophet ﷺ could sit down and give his talk.
- When the Prophet ﷺ started to use the new pulpit, everyone heard the sound of crying. The tree trunk was crying!
- Prophet Muhammad ﷺ made the tree trunk feel better. He gave the tree a choice of either becoming a young tree again or becoming a tree in Paradise. The tree trunk chose to be a tree in Paradise.

15. ANGELS

Lesson Objective: To Understand as Muslims We Believe in Angels.

INSTRUCTIONS: Colour the boxes that describe angels correctly in green and the boxes that do not in red.

Angels are a special creation of Allah ﷾.	Angels do anything they want.
Angels can do bad things.	Angels are Allah's servants.
Angels get married and have a family.	Angels do not eat or drink.
Angels do the jobs that Allah ﷾ tells them to do.	Angels only like good and pure things.

Angels are made from clay.

Angels never make mistakes.

Angels are made from light.

Angels are Allah's daughters.

Angels always listen to Allah سُبْحَانَهُ وَتَعَالَىٰ.

Angels do not listen to Allah سُبْحَانَهُ وَتَعَالَىٰ.

Angels are humans.

Angels have wings.

There are two angels that write our good and bad deeds.

Angels are everywhere and we cannot count them.

INSTRUCTIONS: Match the angel to its job.

Angel Jibra'il

Angel Mika'il

Angel `Izra'il

Angel Israfil

Controlling the weather

Gives Allah's message to the Prophets

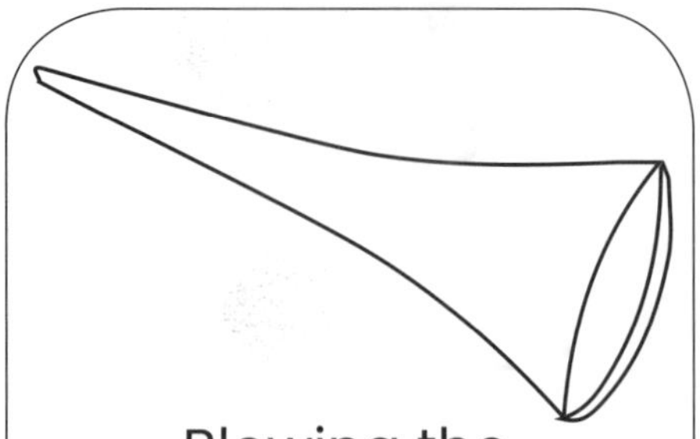

Blowing the trumpet

Taking the soul at the time of death

KEY WORDS

Angels	Light	Wings	Pure
Jibra'il	Mika'il	`Izra'il	Israfil

LESSON SUMMARY

- Muslims believe in angels.
- Angels are a special creation of Allah سبحانه وتعالى. Angels are Allah's servants.
- Angels are made from light and they have wings.
- Angels cannot do what they want. They do the jobs that Allah سبحانه وتعالى tells them to do.
- They always listen to Allah سبحانه وتعالى and they never make mistakes.
- Angels do not eat or drink.
- Angels only like good and pure things.
- The four main Angels are Jibra'il, Mika'il, `Izra'il and Israfil.
- Different angels have different jobs.

16. THE ISLAMIC CALENDAR

Lesson Objective: To Know the Months of the Islamic Calendar.

INSTRUCTIONS: Fill in the gaps using the wordbank below.

The Islamic calendar is called the ______________ calendar. It begins from the time Prophet Muhammed ﷺ travelled from ______________ to ______________.

The Islamic calendar is a ______________ calendar. A lunar calendar is based on the movement of the ______________. The Islamic calendar starts when the ______________ moon can be seen. The lunar month is either ______________ or______________ days.

29	Hijri	Makkah	New
Lunar	Madinah	Moon	30

INSTRUCTIONS: Label thelunar months in the right order. The labels can be found in the cut-out section.

1

2

3

4

5

6

7

8

9

10

11

12

There are _____________ months in the Hijri calendar.

INSTRUCTIONS: Match the dates in the Islamic calendar.

12th Rabi` al-Awwal	Eid al-Fitr
15th Sha`ban	Mawlid an-Nabi (Birth of Prophet Muhammad ﷺ)
27th Ramadan	Eid al-Adha
1st Shawwal	Laylat al-Bara'ah (The Night of Freedom)
9th Dhu al-Hijjah	Laylat al-Qadr (The Night of Power)
10th Dhu al-Hijjah	Yawm al-`Arafah

ACTIVITY

INSTRUCTIONS: Sit in a circle, roll a ball to someone in the circle and say the first month. Then roll the ball again and then say the next month. Continue this until you have completed all twelve months!

KEY WORDS

Hijri	Lunar	Crescent Moon	Eid
Mawlid an-Nabi ﷺ	Laylat al-Qadr	Laylat al-Bara'ah	`Ashura'

LESSON SUMMARY

- There are 12 months in the Hijri calendar.
- The Islamic calendar is called the lunar calendar. It begins from the time Prophet Muhammad ﷺ travelled from Makkah to Madinah.
- The Islamic calendar is a lunar calendar. A lunar calendar is based on the movement of the moon.
- The Islamic calendar starts when the new crescent of the moon can be seen.
- The lunar month is either 29 or 30 days.

17. BEING KIND AND HELPFUL

Lesson Objective: To Understand as Muslims We Must Be Kind and Helpful.

INSTRUCTIONS: Draw three pictures in ways you can be kind and helpful.

☆ ☆ ☆

BE GOOD

☆ ☆ ☆

During Class

During Break Time

☆ ☆ ☆

BE KIND

☆ ☆ ☆

☆ ☆ ☆

BE HELPFUL

☆ ☆ ☆

During Lunch

INSTRUCTIONS: Sort the pictures into the right columns.

BEING KIND AND HELPFUL

NOT BEING KIND AND HELPFUL

KEY WORDS

Kind	Helpful	Sharing	Rewarded
Parents	Teachers	Elders	Friends
Animals	Neighbours	Muslim	Non-Muslim

LESSON SUMMARY

- Be kind and helpful. Allah ﷾ loves those who are kind and helpful to others. The kind and helpful person will be protected from the Hellfire and will be rewarded by Allah ﷾.
- Be kind and helpful to your parents.
- Be kind and helpful to your teacher.
- Be kind and helpful to your elders.
- Be kind and helpful to your friends.
- Be kind and helpful to your neighbours.
- Be kind and helpful to animals.
- Be kind and helpful to everyone, whether they are Muslim or non-Muslim, older than you or younger.

18. PROPHET HUD عليه السلام

Lesson Objective: To Understand the Story of Prophet Hud عليه السلام.

READING COMPREHENSION

Prophet Hud عليه السلام was sent to the people of `Ad. The people of `Ad were rich and powerful. Allah سبحانه وتعالى had made them the strongest people of that time, but they used to worship idols.

1. The people of `Ad were ______________ and ________________.
2. They used to worship ______________.

Prophet Hud عليه السلام told his people that there is only One God, Allah سبحانه وتعالى. He tried to help them by saying, "You should worship the One God, Allah, and not the idols that you make with your own hands. You were made by Allah سبحانه وتعالى and you should be thankful to Him."

3. What did Prophet Hud عليه السلام tell the people?

____

4. Who should we be thankful to?

____

They said to Prophet Hud عليه السلام, "Are you telling us that after we die and turn into dust, we will be brought back to life again?" "Yes. On the Day of Judgement, all of you will be asked about your actions in this life," Prophet Hud عليه السلام replied. They laughed at him and made fun out of him.

5. How did the people react to Prophet Hud عليه السلام?

They listened to him	☐
They walked away	☐
They laughed and made fun of him	☐

Many years passed, and they still did not listen to the message given to them by Prophet Hud عليه السلام. After many years of telling his people to worship Allah سبحانه وتعالى, Prophet Hud عليه السلام warned his people of Allah's punishment. But the people did not care about what Prophet Hud عليه السلام said to them. They just ignored his words and carried on disobeying Allah ﷻ.

6. What did Prophet Hud ﷺ warn the people about?

____

It had not rained for a very long time, so people did not have enough water to drink and there was not enough water for fruits and vegetables to grow. One day, there were dark clouds in the sky. The people got happy seeing the clouds.

7. The people did not have enough water to do which two things?

i.______________________________________

ii.______________________________________

But Prophet Hud ﷺ warned them that this was the punishment of Allah. His people made fun out of him, not believing what he said. As the dark clouds began to come nearer, they also brought a fast and fierce wind with them. There was a storm!

8. What did the dark clouds bring?

A rainbow ☐
A storm ☐
Snow ☐

The storm was so strong that it ripped out trees from the ground and brought down all the tall buildings that were made by the people of `Ad. This wind was so powerful that it destroyed everything. The next morning, when the wind stopped, nothing was left. All the people of `Ad were killed by this powerful storm and they were buried under the sand forever.

9. What did the storm destroy?

____

10. Where was everything buried?

____

INSTRUCTIONS: Draw a picture of the storm and discuss the lesson you learnt from the story of Prophet Hud ﷺ.

KEY WORDS

Sand Dunes	Dark Clouds	Storm	Destroyed
Laugh	Idols	Listen	Warned

LESSON SUMMARY

- Prophet Hud عليه السلام was sent to the people of `Ad. The people of `Ad used to worship idols.
- Prophet Hud عليه السلام told his people that there is only One God, Allah سبحانه وتعالى.
- Over many years, he tried to make them listen. They laughed at him and made fun out of him.
- Many years passed and they still did not listen to the message given to them.
- Prophet Hud عليه السلام warned his people of Allah's punishment. They just ignored his words and carried on disobeying Allah سبحانه وتعالى.
- One day, there were dark clouds in the sky. The people got happy seeing the clouds. But Prophet Hud عليه السلام warned them that this was the punishment of Allah.
- As the dark clouds began to come nearer, they also brought a fast and fierce wind with them. There was a storm!
- All the people of `Ad were killed by this powerful storm and they were buried under the sand forever.

19. THE TRUTHFUL ONE ﷺ

Lesson Objective: To Know that Prophet Muhammed ﷺ was the Truthful One.

INSTRUCTIONS: Read the sentences and number them in the correct order. The first one has been done for you.

When Prophet Muhammad ﷺ was forty years old, he got a special message from Allah سبحانه وتعالى. In this message, Allah سبحانه وتعالى told him to tell others that he was His Prophet and Messenger.	1
Allah سبحانه وتعالى told the Prophet ﷺ to openly tell everyone about Islam. So, the Prophet ﷺ climbed a mountain called Safa and called the people to come and hear what he had to say.	
The people of Makkah came to see what the Prophet ﷺ had to say. They knew the Prophet ﷺ from when he was born. They knew that he would not tell them a lie.	
After receiving the special message, the Prophet ﷺ told his beloved wife Khadijah رضي الله عنها, his best friend Abu Bakr رضي الله عنه and his cousin `Ali رضي الله عنه about it.	
Everyone knew that Prophet Muhammad ﷺ was really a Prophet because he was a truthful man and he would not lie about anything.	
After telling his friends and family, the Prophet ﷺ secretly told people about Islam for three years.	
Prophet Muhammad ﷺ told them, "Listen to me. I have been sent by Allah to warn you and to tell you to worship only Him."	

INSTRUCTIONS: Colour in the words and write a sentence on what truthfulness means.

Truthfulness means:

____

____

INSTRUCTIONS: Write a short story about how you were honest.

INSTRUCTIONS: Put the following sentences in the right column.

- Telling the truth
- Admitting you are wrong
- Telling on someone
- Hiding the truth
- Cheating on a test
- Exaggerating a story
- Telling someone if you saw them doing something wrong
- Telling someone how you feel
- Not telling someone how to do their homework properly

Showing Honesty ☺

1. ______________________________
2. ______________________________
3. ______________________________
4. ______________________________
5. ______________________________
6. ______________________________
7. ______________________________

Not Showing Honesty ☹

1. ______________________________
2. ______________________________
3. ______________________________
4. ______________________________
5. ______________________________
6. ______________________________
7. ______________________________

EXTENSION: If you complete this activity, you can add examples of your own.

ACTIVITY

INSTRUCTIONS: Discuss the story of the boy who cried wolf as a class and the moral of the story.

KEY WORDS

Truthful	Lies	Honesty	Special Message

LESSON SUMMARY

- When Prophet Muhammad ﷺ was forty years old, he got a special message from Allah ﷻ. In this special message, Allah ﷻ told him to tell others that he was His Prophet and Messenger.
- The people of Makkah knew the Prophet ﷺ from when he was born. They knew that he would not tell them a lie. This is why they listened to him and wanted to know what he was going to say.
- Everyone knew that Prophet Muhammad ﷺ was really a Prophet. However, it was only those people who had good hearts who followed Islam and became Muslims straightaway. They knew Islam was a true religion because Prophet Muhammad ﷺ was a truthful man and he would not lie about anything.

20. HOLY BOOKS

Lesson Objective: To Understand as Muslims We Believe in Holy Books.

INSTRUCTIONS: Fill in the blanks.

As Muslims, we believe in the Holy ____________. Allah سبحانه وتعالى sent Holy Books to ______________ people. Allah سبحانه وتعالى gave the Holy Books to the __________________ , and the Prophets gave them to their __________________.

The Holy Books have Allah's special __________________ in them. They tell us to worship __________________ and not to make partners with Him. We must __________________ in the Holy Books.

Prophets	Message	Help
People	Books	Allah
	Believe	

INSTRUCTIONS: Fill in the crossword.

1 down	The Qur'an was given to Prophet ____________________
2 down	The Zabur was given to Prophet ____________________
3 across	The Tawrah was given to Prophet ____________________
4 across	The Injil was given to Prophet ____________________

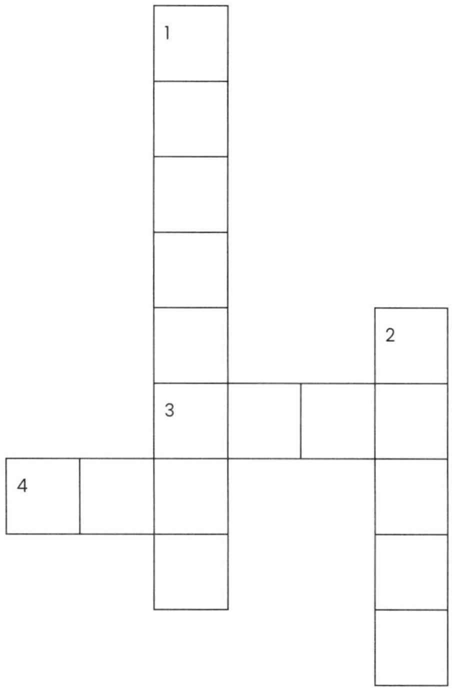

INSTRUCTIONS: Write two facts about the Qur'an and two reasons why you love reading it.

First Fact:

Second Fact:

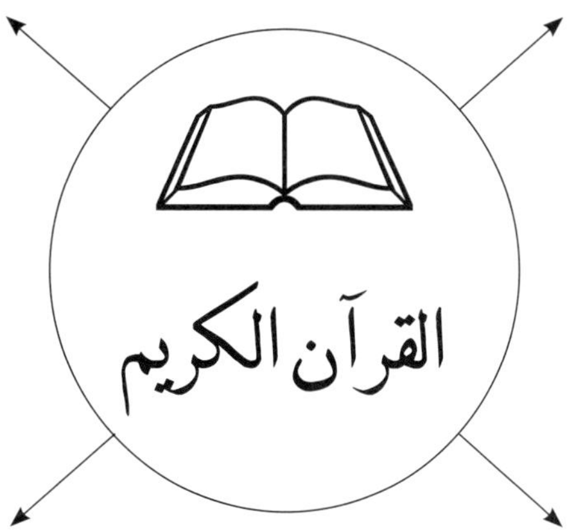

First Reason:

Second Reason:

INSTRUCTIONS: Design your own cover of the Holy Qur’an.

KEY WORDS

Holy Books	Special Message	Believe	Angel Jibra'il
Qur'an	Tawrah	Zabur	Injil

LESSON SUMMARY

- As Muslims, we believe in the Holy Books. Allah ﷻ sent Holy Books to help people. Allah ﷻ gave the Holy Books to the Prophets, and the Prophets gave them to their people.
- The Holy Books have Allah's special message in them. They tell us to worship Allah ﷻ and not to make partners with Him. We must believe in the Holy Books.
- We believe Allah ﷻ sent four holy books.
- The Qur'an is Allah's message given to Prophet Muhammad ﷺ.
- Angel Jibra'il used to bring this message from Allah ﷻ and he gave it to Prophet Muhammad ﷺ little by little over 23 years.
- The Qur'an is the last Holy Book from Allah ﷻ and there will be no Holy Book after it.
- The Qur'an is a miracle of Prophet Muhammad ﷺ

21. FASTING IN RAMADAN

Lesson Objective: To Understand as Muslims We Believe in Holy Books.

INSTRUCTIONS: Match the word to its correct description.

Fasting	The meal we eat when we break the fast after the sun goes down.
Suhur	The special month when we fast. Fasting in this month is a pillar of Islam.
Iftar	When we do not eat or drink during the day.
Ramadan	The meal we eat before the fast.
Tarawih	The Night of Power, when the Qur'an was sent down. It is better than 1000 months.
Laylat al-Qadr	The prayer we offer in the night behind the Imam when we go to the mosque.

INSTRUCTIONS: Write three facts about fasting in Ramadan and fill in the gaps.

Fasting

1.______________________________

____

____

____

in

2.______________________________

____

____

____

Ramadan

3.______________________________

____

____

____

We feel h___________ by fasting and this helps us to know how the p____________ people feel. It teaches us to be k_________ and to think about other p____________.

INSTRUCTIONS: Draw three good things you should do in Ramadan and three things you should not do whilst fasting.

Good ☺	Bad ☹
1.	1.
2.	2.
3.	3.

INSTRUCTIONS: Fill in the gaps using the wordbank below.

In the last ____________ nights of Ramadan, there is a special ___________ called the '_____________________' (Laylat al-Qadr).

This night is better than ____________ months. This night is very ____________ because the ____________ was sent ____________ on this night.

1000	Qur'an	Night
Special	Night of Power	Ten
	Down	

KEY WORDS

Fasting	Ramadan	Suhur	Iftar
Tarawih	Laylat al-Qadr	Kind	Poor

LESSON SUMMARY

- Fasting is when we do not eat or drink during the day. It is a special kind of worship.
- Muslims fast in the month of Ramadan, and it is one of the five pillars of Islam.
- We have a meal before the fast called the 'Suhur'. We break the fast and this meal is called 'Iftar'.
- We feel hungry by fasting and this helps us to know how the poor people feel. It teaches us to be kind and to think about other people.
- During the month of Ramadan, we pray the Tarawih prayer in the night and we go to the mosque to pray this together.
- In the last ten nights of Ramadan, there is a special night called the 'Night of Power' (Laylat al-Qadr).

22. BEING THANKFUL

Lesson Objective: To Understand that We are All Thankful for What Allah ﷻ has Given Us.

INSTRUCTIONS: Write about three things you are thankful for and draw a picture for each.

1. ______________________________

____

____

____

2. ______________________________

____

____

____

3. ______________________________

____

____

____

INSTRUCTIONS: Mention something from each letter of the Alphabet we should be thankful for.

A____________________

B____________________

C____________________

D____________________

E____________________

F____________________

G____________________

H____________________

I____________________

J____________________

K____________________

L____________________

M____________________

N____________________

O____________________

P____________________

Q____________________

R____________________

S____________________

T____________________

U____________________

V____________________

W____________________

X____________________

Y____________________

Z____________________

INSTRUCTIONS: Write a letter thanking someone special. You can draw a picture at the bottom.

ACTIVITY

INSTRUCTIONS: Play the 'Being Thankful' game. Two or more people sit together and sing the following:

Person 1: 'Who forgot to thank Allah سبحانه وتعالى for all His blessing?' [Person 1 picks someone.]

Person 2: 'Who me?'

Person 1: 'Yes, you.'

Person 2: [Thanks Allah سبحانه وتعالى for a blessing.] Person 2 then becomes person 1 and picks someone else. In this way, the game keeps on going.

KEY WORDS

Thankful	Grateful	Blessings	Du`a

LESSON SUMMARY

- We should always thank Allah سبحانه وتعالى for ourselves and Allah's creations.
- Allah سبحانه وتعالى has given us so many blessings that we should be thankful to Him.
- We should make du`a and try to help the poor people.
- We should be thankful to Allah سبحانه وتعالى that He blessed us with so many nice things. If we are thankful, Allah سبحانه وتعالى will give us more. We should not be ungrateful to Him.
- We should also be thankful to other people as well.
- Be thankful to your parents.
- Be thankful to your teachers, whether they are Muslims or not. Listen to them and show them respect.

23. PROPHET SALIH عليه السلام

Lesson Objective: To Understand the Story of Prophet Salih عليه السلام.

READING COMPREHENSION

1. Match the sentences:

Prophet Salih عليه السلام was sent to ...	... worship Allah سبحانه وتعالى.
Prophet Salih عليه السلام reminded his people to ...	... but they challenged him instead.
Prophet Salih عليه السلام carried on telling the people to worship Allah سبحانه وتعالى ...	... the people of Thamud.

2. The people asked, "Show us a sign that you are truly the Prophet of Allah and are speaking the truth." What sign did they ask Prophet Salih عليه السلام for?

3. Why did the people of Thamud ask Prophet Salih عليه السلام to do this very hard task?

They wanted to eat the she-camel ☐
They believed that he could not do it ☐
They were playing a game ☐

4. Did the people promise to believe in Prophet Salih عليه السلام if he performed this miracle?

Yes ☐

No ☐

5. After seeing the miracle, what did most of the people do?

____

____

6. Fill in the missing words using the wordbank.

Everyone got their ______________ from a well. Prophet Salih عليه السلام told the people to let the ______________ drink from the water well on ______________ day and then they could drink from it the ______________ day. The people did not ______________ this idea and after some time they decided to ______________ the she-camel.

Like	Next	Water
One	Kill	She-Camel

7. How do you think Prophet Salih عليه السلام felt when he found out some men killed the she-camel?

____

8. When Prophet Salih عليه السلام told the people, "Ask for forgiveness from Allah. If you do not, then you will get Allah's punishment," what did his people do to him?

They listened to what he said ☐

They laughed at him and did not care ☐

They stopped speaking to him ☐

9. Prophet Salih ﷺ and his small group of followers left the people of Thamud and went somewhere else. Write a sentence about what happened when they left?

____

____

____

INSTRUCTIONS: Colour in the picture and write two words to describe the she-camel.

1. ____________________ 2. ____________________

ACTIVITY

INSTRUCTIONS: Discuss as a class the key points from the lesson.

KEY WORDS

She-Camel	Thamud	Challenge	Water Well

LESSON SUMMARY

- Prophet Salih عليه السلام was sent to the people of Thamud. He reminded them to worship only Allah سبحانه وتعالى.
- The people challenged him. So, Prophet Salih عليه السلام prayed to Allah to show the people a miracle.
- The rock split apart and a tall, beautiful she-camel came walking out of the rock.
- Despite seeing this great miracle, most of the people still did not want to believe.
- One day, while the camel was in the field, some young men came and killed the she-camel. Prophet Salih عليه السلام was very sad when he found out about this.
- Prophet Salih عليه السلام told the people to ask Allah سبحانه وتعالى for forgiveness. The people did not listen.
- After three days, while the people were sleeping in their homes, Allah سبحانه وتعالى sent a powerful earthquake and fierce winds.

24. LIFE AFTER DEATH

Lesson Objective: To Understand What Life After Death Is.

INSTRUCTIONS: Match the sentences in both columns.

This life is ...	... when Allah سبحانه وتعالى brings us back to life again.
Life after death is ...	... the last day when this world will end.
The Day of Judgement is ...	... a test to see who is good and who is bad.
On the Day of Judgement ...	... we will go to a special place called Paradise (Jannah).
If we were good in this life ...	... we will go to a horrible place called Hell (Jahannum).
If we were bad in this life ...	... our actions will be measured on a big scale.

INSTRUCTIONS: Answer the questions and fill in the blanks.

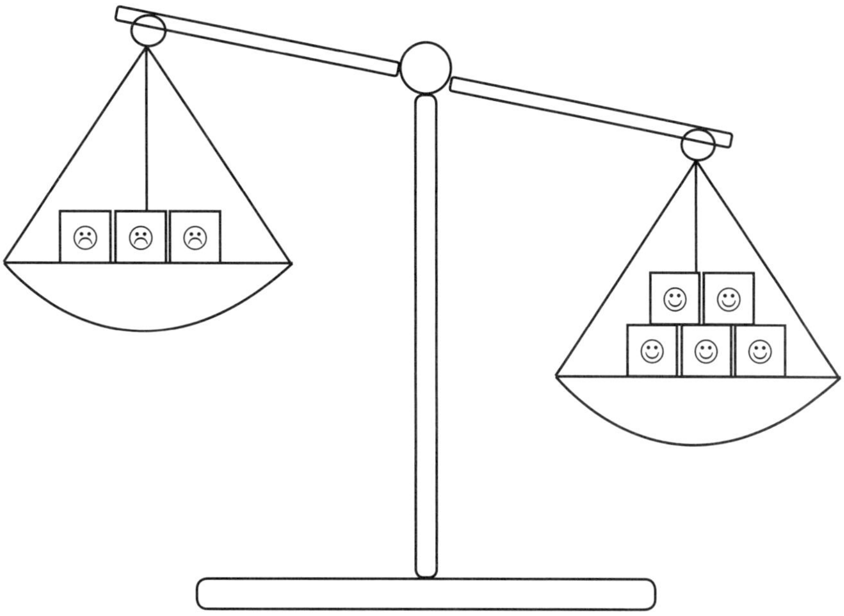

Bad Actions:

1. ______________________________
2. ______________________________
3. ______________________________

Good Actions:

1. ______________________________
2. ______________________________
3. ______________________________
4. ______________________________
5. ______________________________

Which side of the scale is heavier?

The good actions ☐

The bad actions ☐

If our ______________ actions are heavier than our bad actions, we will go to a place called ______________, but if our ______________ actions are heavier than our good actions, we will go to a place called ______________.

INSTRUCTIONS: From the cut out section, place the actions in the right column.

Paradise (Jannah) ☺	Hell (Jahannum) ☹

KEY WORDS

Good Actions	Bad Actions	Scale	Life After Death
Day of Judgement	Paradise (Jannah)	Hell (Jahannum)	Test

LESSON SUMMARY

- We were made by Allah سبحانه وتعالى to worship and obey Him.
- This life is a test to see who is good and who is bad.
- After death, Allah سبحانه وتعالى will bring us back to life again. We will be given a new life, and this is called 'life after death'.
- The last day is called the 'Day of Judgement'. On this day, Allah سبحانه وتعالى will look at all our actions that we did in this life.
- If we are good, we will be rewarded for our good deeds. If we are bad, we will be punished for our bad deeds.
- On the Day of Judgement, our actions will be measured on a big scale.
- If our good actions are heavier than our bad actions, we will go to a special place called Paradise (Jannah).
- If our bad actions are heavier than our good actions, we will go to a horrible place called Hell (Jahannum)

25. ZAKAH AND SADAQAH

Lesson Objective: To Understand that Giving Charity is Important for Muslims.

INSTRUCTIONS: Fill in the blanks using the wordbank below.

The Arabic word for charity is ________________. Sadaqah is one way to ________________ the poor people or anyone else who needs our help. ________________ tells us to help the poor and to ________________ after them.

The ________________ people, ________________ people and ________________ also need our help. Charity is a good way to make sure everyone gets what they ________________ so that no one is left poor and ________________.

Old	Allah	Homeless
Sadaqah	Need	Orphans
Help	Look	Hungry

INSTRUCTIONS: Write a sentence about Zakah and why it is different from Sadaqah.

____

____

____

INSTRUCTIONS: Give four examples of acts of charity (Sadaqah) other than giving money to the poor and needy. Draw a picture for each example.

1.________________________

2.________________________

3.________________________

4.________________________

KEY WORDS

Sadaqah	Charity	Poor	Help
Sharing	Kind	Zakat	Pillar of Islam

LESSON SUMMARY

- The Arabic word for charity is Sadaqah. Giving charity (Sadaqah) is a very important part of being a Muslim.
- Charity is one of the ways to help the poor people or anyone else who needs our help. It is a good way to make sure that everyone gets what they need so that no one is poor or hungry.
- Sadaqah makes us think about other people and be generous to them. Giving charity is a way of thanking Allah ﷻ. We should do acts of charity every day by being kind and helpful to other people.
- Giving a small amount of money every year is called Zakah, and it is one of the pillars of Islam.

26. BEING HONEST

Lesson Objective: To Understand That We Should Always Tell the Truth.

INSTRUCTIONS: Answer the questions.

1. What three things shows you are honest?

i.____

ii.____

iii.____

2. How do you feel when someone tells a lie?

____

____

3. Why is it important not to lie?

____

____

4. Write three classroom rules that will help everyone to be honest:

i.____

ii.____

iii.____

5. What do you think should happen if we are not honest in class?

____

____

6. Write about the time when you were honest?

____

____

INSTRUCTIONS: Draw two pictures that show someone being dishonest and write a sentence about what you have drawn.

1.______________________________

____

____

____

2.______________________________

____

____

____

KEY WORDS

Truth	Lying	Stealing	Permission

LESSON SUMMARY

- We should always tell the truth. Prophet Muhammad ﷺ always spoke the truth. He was known as 'as-Sadiq' (the truthful) and 'al-Amin' (the trustworthy).
- Lying is a very big sin. Allah ﷻ does not like people who lie.
- Do not steal. Stealing is when you take something that is not yours. Ask for permission before taking anything that belongs to other people.
- Be honest with everyone. Do not behave badly with someone just because they are different to you.
- If someone asks you to look after their things, you should take care of them.
- If someone tells you a secret, do not tell other people the secret.
- When it is time for learning, you should stop playing and learn. If we play when it is learning time, then we are not being honest.

27. THE COMPANIONS OF THE CAVE

Lesson Objective: To Understand the Story of the Companions of the Cave.

INSTRUCTIONS: Put the story of the Companions of the Cave in the correct order and draw a picture for each part of the story. The storyboard can be found in the cut-out section.

1

2

3

4

5

6

7	
8	
9	

INSTRUCTIONS: Draw a picture of the cave and the beautiful mosque at the mouth of the cave.

Allah سبحانه وتعالى made the men sleep for __________ years!

KEY WORDS

Evil King	Idols	Young Men	Dog
Cave	Sleep	Coins	Mosque

LESSON SUMMARY

- There were seven young men who worshipped Allah سبحانه وتعالى. They told the evil king not to worship idols.
- The evil king did not like this, and he ordered his soldiers to capture the young men.
- The seven young men escaped and hid in a cave. Their dog followed them to the cave and stayed with them.
- They slept in the cave for 309 years.
- After waking up, they used old coins to buy food and everyone realised they were the seven young men who left their town 309 years ago.
- The seven young men saw how people did not worship idols anymore.
- When they died, they were buried in the cave and some good people built a mosque at the mouth of the cave to get blessings.

28. PARADISE AND HELL

Lesson Objective: To Understand that Allah سبحانه وتعالى made Paradise and Hell.

INSTRUCTIONS: Put the following sentences in the right box.

- Good people will be sent here
- It is a horrible place
- Bad people will be sent here as punishment
- You will live happily forever
- You will get anything you want
- It is a very big fire
- We cannot imagine how beautiful this place is
- When Allah سبحانه وتعالى decides, He will take them out of here
- It is a reward for being good
- The people who did not listen to Allah سبحانه وتعالى will be here

Paradise (Jannah) ☺

1. ______________________________
2. ______________________________
3. ______________________________
4. ______________________________
5. ______________________________

Hell (Jahannum) ☹

1. ______________________________
2. ______________________________
3. ______________________________
4. ______________________________
5. ______________________________

INSTRUCTIONS: Draw the things you think you might see in Paradise and Hell.

Paradise (Jannah) ☺	Hell (Jahannum) ☹

KEY WORDS

Paradise (Jannah)	Hell (Jahannam)	Good	Bad

LESSON SUMMARY

- Allah ﷾ made Paradise (Jannah) and Hell (Jahannam).
- After Judgement Day, people will be sent to either Paradise (Jannah) or Hell (Jahannam).
- Good people will be sent to Paradise (Jannah). They will live there forever. It is a reward for being good in this life.
- Bad people will be sent to Hell (Jahannam). It is a horrible place. Those people who did not listen to Allah ﷾ in this life and were cruel will be sent to Hell as a punishment.

29. HAJJ AND ZIYARAH

Lesson Objective: To Understand that Makkah and Madinah are Special Places that Muslims Visit.

INSTRUCTIONS: Produce a story map of the journey to Makkah and Madinah. Underneath each picture, write a sentence to describe the picture.

INSTRUCTIONS: Fill in the gaps and match the words to the pictures.

The Hajj is a s_______________ journey a Muslim goes on to visit M_______________. It is one of the f_______________ pillars of Islam. As Muslims, we must perform Hajj at least o_______________ in our life, if we can. A person who goes to Makkah to perform the Hajj is called a p______________.

Ihram

Zamzam

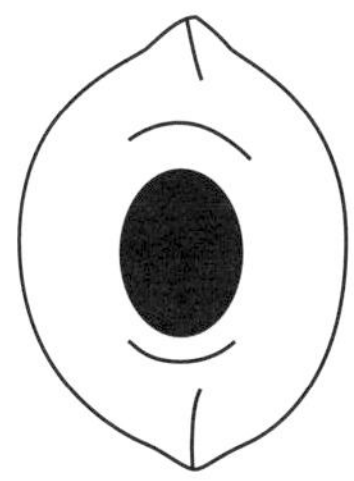

Tawaf

Blackstone

Safa and Marwah

INSTRUCTIONS: Identify the following from their description.

A white cloth worn during `Umrah and Hajj

A: ______________________________

The special stone in the corner of the Ka`bah

A: ______________________________

Special water from a well

A: ______________________________

Going around the Ka`bah seven times

A: ______________________________

The two mountains that Hajrah ﷺ ran between seven times

A: ______________________________

INSTRUCTIONS: Answer the following questions.

1. Who is buried in Madinah?

____

2. The Prophet's Mosque is called?

Al-Aqsa ☐
Ka`bah ☐
Masjid an-Nabawi ☐

3. Inside the Mosque is the Prophet's grave. This special place is called?

____

4. Next to the Prophet's grave is a special place called 'Riyad al-Jannah'. What do the words 'Riyad al-Jannah' mean?

____

5. Write down two actions we can do whilst in Madinah?

i.____

ii.____

KEY WORDS

Hajj	Ziyarah	Makkah	Madinah
Ihram	Tawaf	Safa	Marwah
Blackstone	Zamzam	Rawdah	Riyad al-Jannah

LESSON SUMMARY

- The Hajj is a special journey a Muslim goes on to visit Makkah. It is one of the five pillars of Islam.
- A person who goes to Makkah to perform the Hajj is called a pilgrim. The pilgrim wears two white sheets called an Ihram. He walks around the Ka`bah seven times. This is called the Tawaf.
- In the corner of the Ka`bah, there is a special stone from Paradise (Jannah). This stone is called al-Hajar al-Aswad (the Black Stone). There is a water-well underground next to the Ka'bah called Zamzam. The pilgrims drink its holy water.
- There are two small mountains near the Ka`bah. They are called Safa and Marwah. The pilgrims run between these two mountains.
- Madinah is where Prophet Muhammad ﷺ is buried. Visiting Madinah before or after the Hajj is called Ziyarah.
- The Prophet's mosque is in Madinah. It is called Masjid an-Nabawi. Inside the Prophet's mosque is the grave of Prophet Muhammad ﷺ. It is in a place called the Rawdah.
- Next to the Prophet's grave is Riyad al-Jannah (the Garden of Paradise).

30. THE SIRAH TIMELINE

Lesson Objective: To Understand that the Sirah Timeline Highlights Special Events in the Life of Prophet Muhammad ﷺ.

INSTRUCTIONS: Make a timeline about five important events in your life. You should write a sentence and draw a picture for each. You can also mention your age during each event.

INSTRUCTIONS: Complete the Sirah timeline using the following points.

- Journey to Abyssinia
- The first revelation in the cave of Hira'
- The treaty of Hudaybiyah
- The farewell pilgrimage
- End of the boycott, the Year of Sorrow and the Night Journey and Heavenly Journey
- Journey to Syria and meeting with Bahirah, the monk.

EXTENSION: If you complete this activity, you can add the Prophet's age to each part of the timeline.

Born in Makkah on the 12th of Rabi` al-Awwal.

____

____

The business trip to Syria and marriage to Lady Khadijah ﵂.

Rebuilding the Ka`bah and placing the Blackstone in its corner.

____

____

Telling people about Islam openly.

____

The boycott and the retreat to the mountain pass of Abu Talib.

____

____

The journey to Madinah and the building of the Prophet's mosque.

The Battles of Badr, Uhud and Khandaq.

____

Conquests of Khaybar and Makkah.

____

The Prophet ﷺ passed away.

INSTRUCTIONS: Complete the quiz.

1. Where was Prophet Muhammad ﷺ born?

Makkah ☐
Madinah ☐
Quds ☐

2. Which Islamic month was the Prophet Muhammad ﷺ born in?

Ramadan ☐
Safar ☐
Rabi` al-Awwal ☐

3. How old was Prophet Muhammad ﷺ when he married Khadijah رضي الله عنها?

40 ☐
25 ☐
30 ☐

4. In which cave did the Prophet ﷺ receive the first revelation?

Tur ☐
Hira' ☐
Uhud ☐

5. In which city did the Prophet ﷺ build his mosque?

Makkah ☐
Madinah ☐
Quds ☐

6. What was the first battle fought by Muslims?

Badr ☐
Uhud ☐
Khandaq (Trenches) ☐

7. At what age did Prophet Muhammad ﷺ pass away?

53 ☐
60 ☐
63 ☐

31. STAYING HEALTHY

Lesson Objective: To Understand that Keeping Healthy Means Looking After Our Health.

INSTRUCTIONS: Draw and label five healthy foods and five unhealthy foods.

Healthy Foods ☺	Unhealthy Foods ☹

INSTRUCTIONS: Draw a healthy food plate. Then write a short paragraph explaining what food you have chosen and why you have chosen to put it on your healthy food plate.

INSTRUCTIONS: Fill in the gaps and draw and label three different ways to stay healthy besides eating healthy food.

We should look after our __________. It is a great blessing from __________. We should be _____________ to Allah ﷻ for our good health.

1. ____

2. ____

3. ____

ACTIVITY

INSTRUCTIONS: Make a list of the Prophet's favourite foods and discuss the different sport activities Prophet Muhammad ﷺ enjoyed. Organise a fun day to compete in these activities!

KEY WORDS

Health	Thankful	Fruit	Vegetables
Active	Unhealthy	Sugar	Junk

LESSON SUMMARY

- We should look after our health. It is a great blessing from Allah ﷻ.
- Allah ﷻ made our bodies for us so that we could do good actions.
- Stay away from bad eating habits.
- Stay away from unhealthy foods and snacks.
- Eat less junk food and more fruits and vegetables.
- Stay away from fast food and fried foods. This type of food is not good for you.
- You should be active and fit.

32. RESPECTING THE QUR'AN

Lesson Objective: To Understand that We Show Respect to the Qur'an.

INSTRUCTIONS: Fill in the blanks using the wordbank below.

As Muslims, we respect the Qur'an because every ____________ in the Qur'an is from Allah ﷻ. We show ____________ to the Qur'an by putting it in a ____________ place. We keep it wrapped up in a clean cover or cloth and we do not put our ____________ towards it.

We should not put other ____________ or anything else on ____________ of it. We never put the Qur'an on the ____________ because this is disrespectful and very ____________. We always keep the Qur'an higher than everything else.

Feet	Top	Respect	Bad
Word	Floor	Clean	Books

Can you think of three other ways we should respect the Qur'an?

1.____

2.____

3.____

INSTRUCTIONS: Write about how the Qur'an is special to you and draw a picture to show how you feel.

INSTRUCTIONS: Colour in the English and Arabic texts and write down the English translation.

BEFORE WE START READING THE QUR'AN, WE SAY:

Ta`awwudh (Seeking Refuge from Shaytan)

أَعُوْذُ بِاللّٰهِ مِنَ الشَّيْطَانِ الرَّجِيْمِ

____

____

____

Tasmiyah (Beginning with Allah's Name)

بِسْمِ اللّٰهِ الرَّحْمٰنِ الرَّحِيْمِ

____

____

____

EXTENSION: Memorise the Arabic text and the English translation.

KEY WORDS

Qur’an	Respect	Special	Disrespectful
Clean	Wudu’	Qiblah	Floor

LESSON SUMMARY

- As Muslims, we respect the Qur’an because every word in the Qur’an is from Allah سبحانه وتعالى.
- We show respect to the Qur’an by putting it in a special place. We keep it wrapped up in a clean cover or cloth and we do not put our feet towards it. We should not put other books or anything else on top of the Qur’an.
- We never put the Qur’an on the floor because this is disrespectful and very bad. We always keep the Qur’an higher than everything else.
- When we read the Qur’an, we should not talk to other people.
- We should try to read the Qur’an in a beautiful voice. Do not rush when you are reading it.
- If someone else is reading the Qur’an loudly, listen to it silently.

LESSON 3: KEEPING SAFE

INSTRUCTIONS: Cut out the following pictures for lesson 3.

LESSON 3: KEEPING SAFE

INSTRUCTIONS: Cut out the following pictures for lesson 3.

LESSON 11: THE SALAH (PRAYER)

INSTRUCTIONS: Cut out the following images for lesson 11.

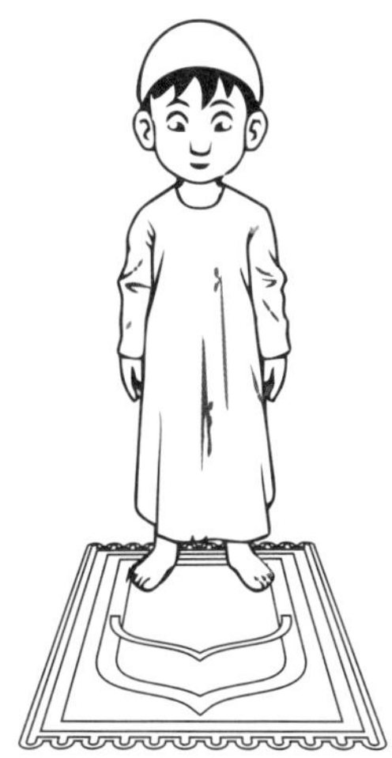

LESSON 11: THE SALAH (PRAYER)

INSTRUCTIONS: Cut out the following images for lesson 11.

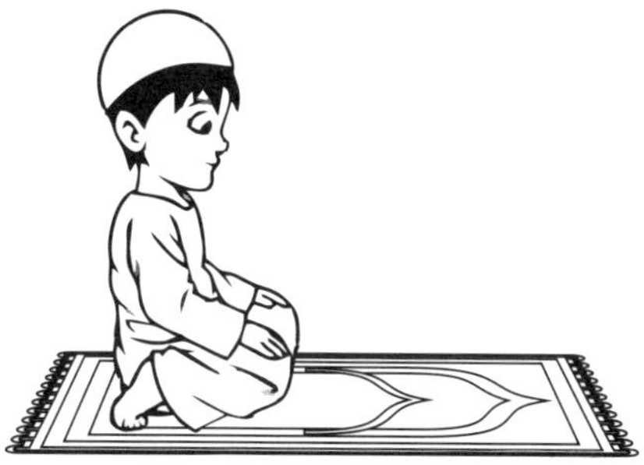

LESSON 13: THE STORY OF `UZAYR ﷺ

INSTRUCTIONS: Cut out the following text for the storyboard in lesson 13.

`Uzayr ﷺ sat under the tree and wondered what happened to this place?	After 100 years the same place was busy and lots of people lived there.
"This place is so empty and broken. How will Allah ﷻ make this busy and full of life again," `Uzayr ﷺ said.	Allah ﷻ sent another angel to bring him back to life. The angel told `Uzayr ﷺ he was asleep for 100 years.
As soon as `Uzayr ﷺ said these words, Allah ﷻ sent the angel of death to take his life.	He was shocked. His food was still fresh. He was amazed at the power of Allah ﷻ.

LESSON 16: THE ISLAMIC CALENDAR

INSTRUCTIONS: Cut out the following boxes for the activity in lesson 16. You can colour in the Arabic text first before cutting them out.

Muharram

Safar

Rabi` al-Awwal

Rabi` ath-Thani

Jumada al-'Ula

Jumada al-Ukhra

Rajab

Sha`ban

Ramadan

Shawwal

Dhu al-Qa`dah

Dhu al-Hijjah

LESSON 17: BEING KIND AND HELPFUL

INSTRUCTIONS: Draw a picture for each of the descriptions and sort them out into the right columns.

Helping the teacher with books.

Giving some food to a cat or dog.

Giving a chair to an elderly person.

Helping a neighbour with gardening.

Helping one's parents with housework.

LESSON 17: BEING KIND AND HELPFUL

INSTRUCTIONS: Draw a picture for each of the descriptions and sort them out into the right columns.

Sharpening a pencil on the classroom floor.	
Throwing stones at a cat or dog.	
Not giving up one's seat to an elderly person.	
Throwing rubbish in someone's garden.	
Scribbling on the wall.	

LESSON 24: LIFE AFTER DEATH

INSTRUCTIONS: Cut out the labels for the activity in lesson 24.

Helping others	Saying bad words
Being nice and kind	Bullying others
Praying and fasting	Not praying or fasting
Giving charity	Not sharing
Giving a gift to someone	Being greedy
Feeding animals	Hurting animals
Reading and learning	Not doing homework
Respecting parents	Not respecting teachers

27. THE COMPANIONS OF THE CAVE

INSTRUCTIONS: Cut out the following text for the storyboard in lesson 27.

There lived an evil king. He made his people worship idols even if they did not want to.

From his people there were seven young men who believed in Allah ﷻ. They did not worship idols.

One day, the seven young men decided to tell the king in front of all the people that they believed in Allah ﷻ and did not worship idols.

This king did not like this so he ordered for them to be locked up. The seven young men escaped and hid inside a cave with their dog.

The seven young men slept in the cave for 309 years. Their dog slept in the cave with them.

When they woke up, they felt hungry. So one of them went to the town to buy some food.

27. THE COMPANIONS OF THE CAVE

INSTRUCTIONS: Cut out the following text for the storyboard in lesson 27.

The coins the man had used were very old, and everyone realised that they were the seven young men who left 309 years ago.

The young men saw that the people had changed and they did not worship idols anymore.

When the young men died, they were buried in the cave and some good people built a mosque there to get blessings.